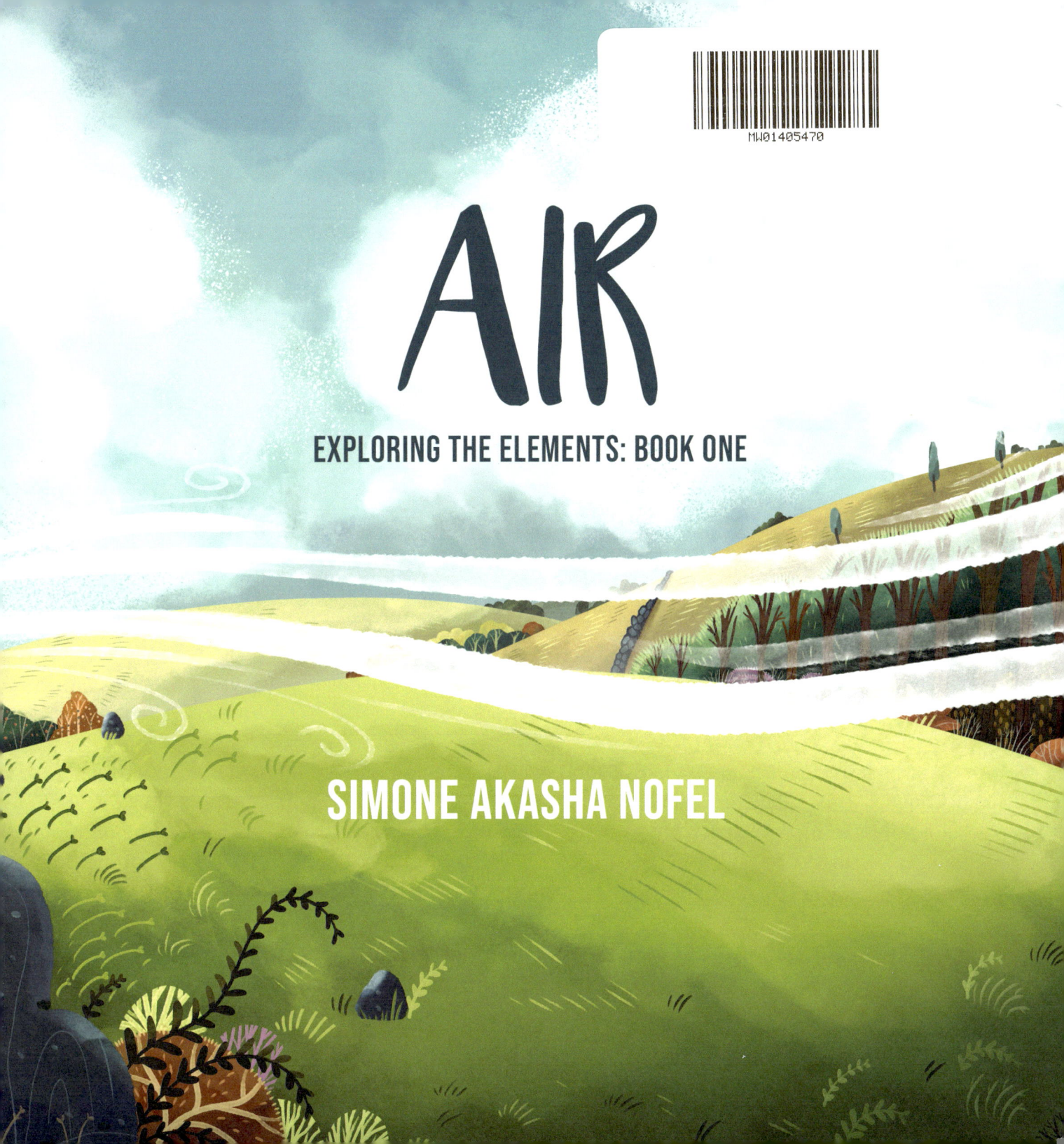

For my son, Destin Ryker.
Always remember, the universe is your playground!

And for you - the reader
Keep exploring, creating, and loving!

Air© Copyright <<November 2021>> Simone Nofel
Place of Publication, Seattle, WA

Book cover design, illustration, editing, and interior layout by:

www.1000storybooks.com

All rights reserved under the International and Pan-American Copyright Conventions. No part of this book may be reproduced or transmitted in any form or by any means, electronic or mechanical, including photocopying and recording, or by any information storage and retrieval system, without permission in writing from publisher.

The advice and strategies found within may not be suitable for every situation. This work is sold with the understanding that neither the author nor the publisher are held responsible for the results accrued from the advice in this book.

Warning: the unauthorized reproduction or distribution of this copyrighted work is illegal. Criminal copyright infringement, including infringement without monetary gain, is investigated by the FBI and is punishable by up to 5 years in prison and a fine of $250,000.

For more information, email support@heartyandfree.com

Paperback ISBN: 978-1-957327-01-3

Hardcover ISBN: 978-1-957327-00-6

eBook ISBN: 978-1-957327-02-0

Library of Congress Control Number: 2022900983

BEFORE YOU READ:

Sit outside if you can, or near a window inside.

Take a deep breath.

I am Air. I am the element that is in constant motion, always on the move.

I am the wind that blows through the trees, shaking all the leaves. You can also feel me as a gentle breeze through your hair.

With a gust of wind, I help flowers pollinate. Pollen can travel great distances on a windy day.

With a breeze, I also help fungi spores disperse.

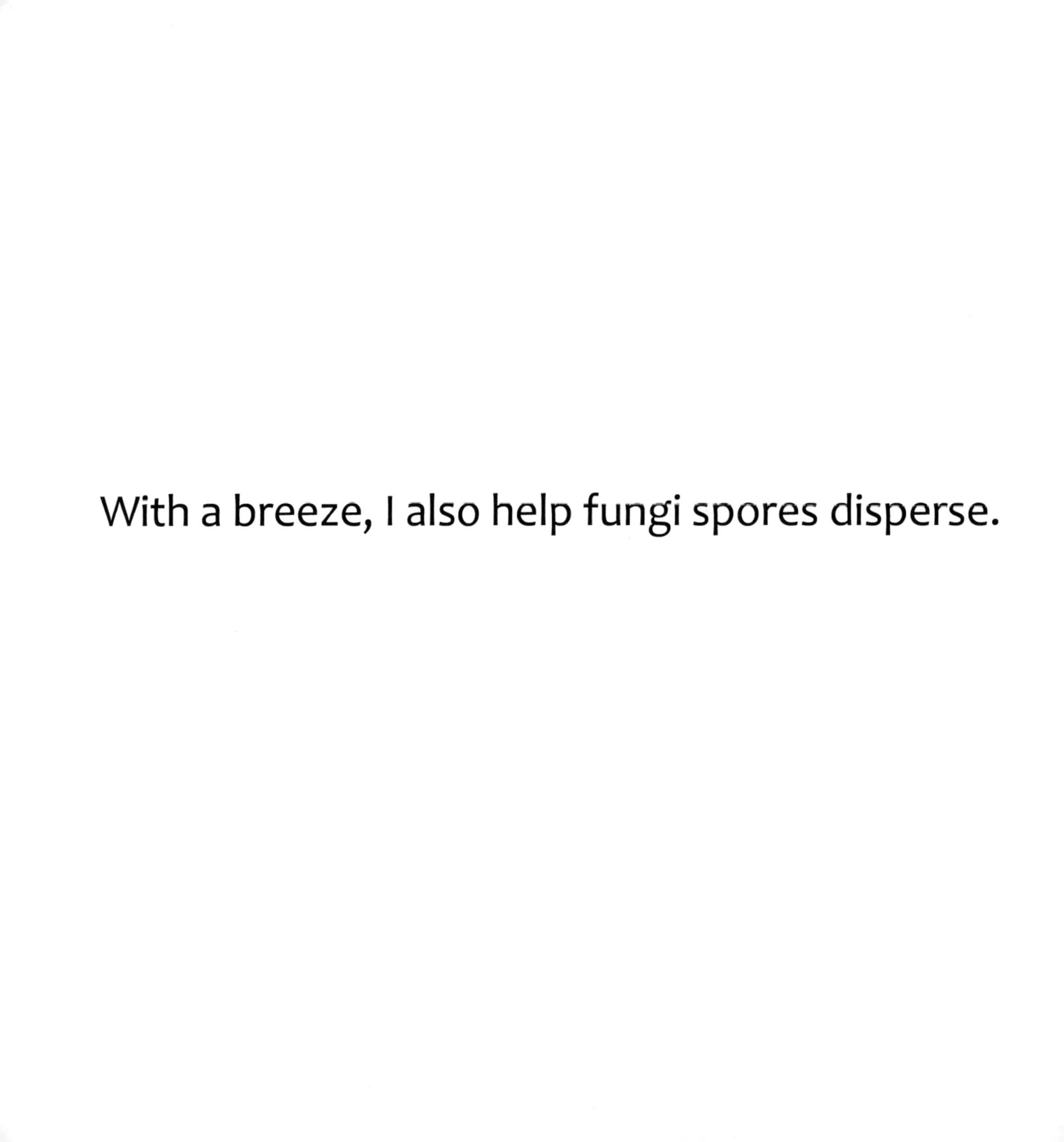

Spores fall from mushrooms and get carried along in the wind to find new places to grow.

I am the reason you breathe. I help oxygen flow into your lungs with each inhale.

I also help you speak, sing, laugh, and shout.

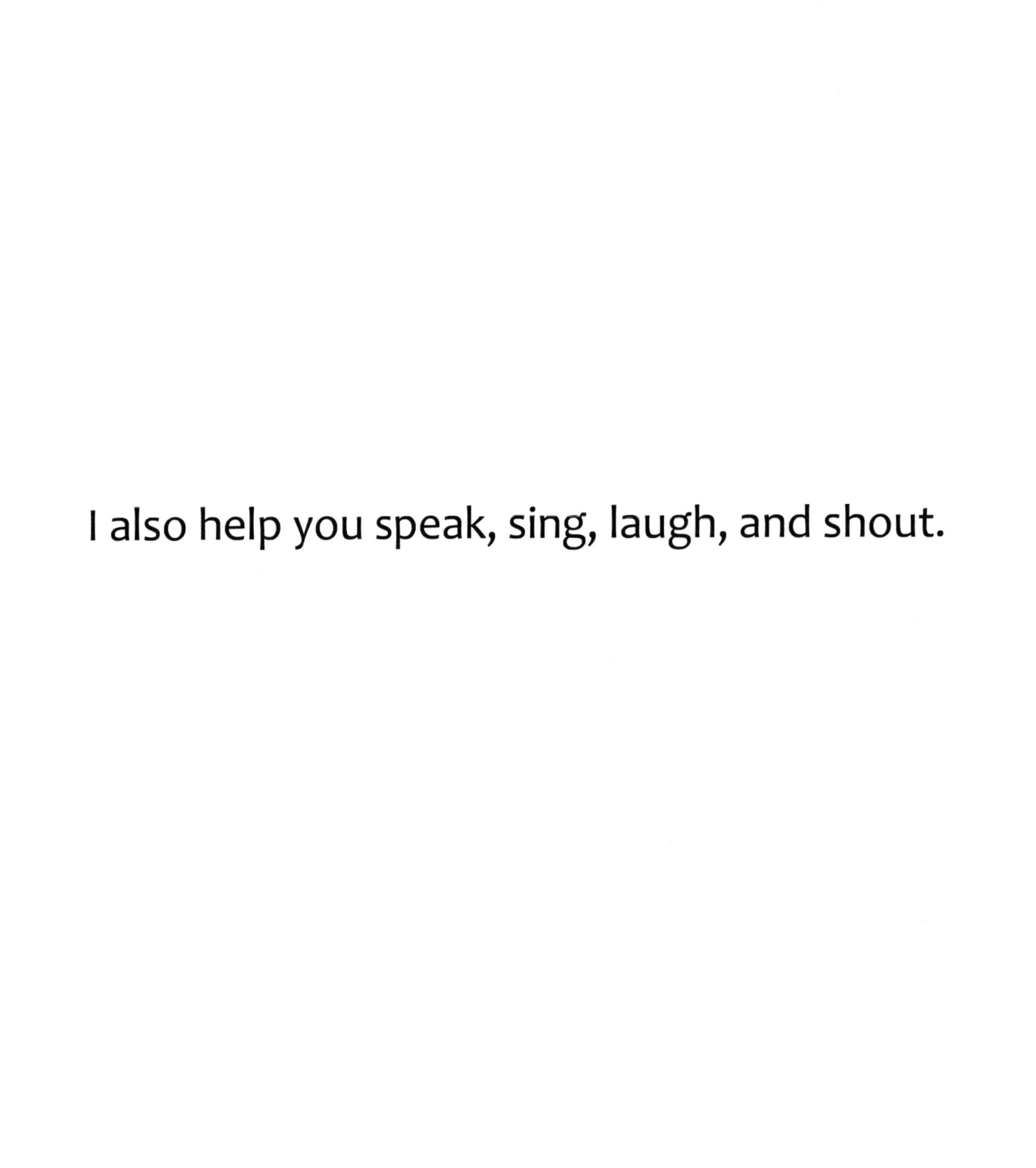

I flow throughout your body as oxygenated blood. I leave your body as carbon dioxide waste with each exhale.

Please help keep me pure for you and other animals to breathe. Protecting coral reefs, planting trees, and learning about soil health are the best ways to help.

Caution! Watch out if you see me form a funnel as a stormy tornado!

FUN FACTS!

- I represent communication, movement, breath, and clarity.

- I am paired with the color yellow.

- My common symbols are:

SUGGESTED ACTIVITIES
(ASK YOUR GROWN-UP FOR HELP)

You can visually experience Air by watching how steam and smoke form. How?

- Boil Water
- Burn Sage

You can watch me blow objects around by flying kites or crafting pinwheels.

- To learn how to make kites and pinwheels with full instructions, visit heartyandfree.com/4kids

To watch pre-recorded breathwork exercises, visit heartyandfree.com/4kids

Find more fun at heartyandfree.com/4kids

COMING SOON...

Fire | Water | Earth | Ether |

Check heartyandfree.com/4kids for latest releases!

LOVE THIS BOOK?
DON'T FORGET TO LEAVE A REVIEW!

Every review matters, and it matters a lot!

Head over to Amazon or wherever you purchased this book to leave a review for me.

My heart thanks you!

Made in United States
Troutdale, OR
02/14/2024

17630466R00017